THE PELT OF WASPS

DAVID CONSTANTINE

THE
Pelt
OF
Wasps

BLOODAXE BOOKS

ISBN: 1 85224 428 3

First published 1998 by
Bloodaxe Books Ltd,
P.O. Box 1SN,
Newcastle upon Tyne NE99 1SN.

Bloodaxe Books Ltd acknowledges
the financial assistance of Northern Arts.

Cover printing by J. Thomson Colour Printers Ltd, Glasgow.

Printed in Great Britain by
Cromwell Press Ltd, Broughton Gifford, Melksham, Wiltshire.

for my brother Steve
and in memory of his wife Wendy

Acknowledgements

Acknowledgements are due to the editors of the following magazines and anthologies in which some of these poems were first published or were reprinted: *Blue Nose Poetry Anthology* (Blue Nose Poets, 1993), *College Green, Departures, The Forward Book of Poetry 1997* (Forward Publishing, 1996), *North, The Orange Dove of Fiji, The New Republic, Orbis, Oxford Poetry, PN Review, Poetry Review, Poetry Wales, The Rialto, Stand, Tabla,* and *The Times Literary Supplement.*

'Soldiering On' was commissioned for St Margaret's Hospital, Swindon, by Southern Arts and Age Concern. It was broadcast, along with 'Cycladic Idols' and 'Quaker Memorial Meeting', on Radio 3 in November 1996.

Lady Hamilton and the Elephant Man was first published in *PN Review*, and an abridged version was broadcast on Radio 3 in February 1997.

Contents

Piers

A jetty is a brave thought
And a pier a cheerful hubris
Going in deeper and deeper to stay level

It carries the fairground far out. Lovers need a pier
To pace out the new extent of themselves
And learn what they are risking.

At low tide the legs of a pier
Are as shocking as the veined white legs of the fathers.
In the stink, under the decking, in the belly of the whale

You saw the red cigarette-ends of the numbered soldiers
Courting. You see the aged
Wheeling eagerly out to the fishermen and the broken-hearted

Out to the limits of the pier, still pointing.

Returns

Returns: as when
That evening in summer on a sunny breeze
The Atlantic entered

A drop, one silver bead,
Out of it opening a whole water
Out of it flowering and relaxing over the patience of the flats

And the gladness of the salt-loving lives was palpable,
What could was floated, the carcasses
Were at a depth, the veins

Were filled, and we
In a room on a jut of land with a window out,
A captain's window, sea three sides the bed,

Into the chuckling sea we pushed our cries.

The Mirror

Mirror, the window set
On a sharp starlight and the moon ascending
Flat, like a shark. Out of her clothes,

Membra disjecta on their battleground,
All the warmth has gone. He puts his hopes
In cold, expends

His wishes on her glass. Remembering
The silk slide from her shoulders as quickly as mercury
He knows his heart must fall a floor like a lift

And in that loss of heat she will precipitate
As white as flour. The shock,
The sigh, as though his eyes,

Hard on her fingertips, were being put out.

The Apple Tree

Night gone and the dream is stranded
Or this is a bold dream that has stepped some paces forward
The apple tree in a startling frost

Faces the sun in a clothing from elsewhere
Crackles with a freezing fire. There are no proofs
Only these goadings. The frost

Rasped like a cat's tongue at the windowpanes.
She entered suddenly with all her clothes in a bundle
Backing the door to threw the bundle down.

Waking I remember the ha'pennies
I warmed as a child and laid against the frost
To see. I watch the bright grey apple tree

Slowly denuding, slowly vanishing.

Peacock

A man's fist may be very gentle
When he takes a butterfly off the pane
And feels the tickle of her wings like desperate eyes.

She seemed to know what she wanted.
Bodily she made the sign of it against the glass,
Sign of her need, sign of the impediment.

October again. The wind.
The trees gasp and are suddenly naked
And everything whirled in the air is dead or dying.

She had opened like an illumination
Under the wall-lamp above their pillow
Still as a brooch, and the savage wind at the pane.

Eyes in the dark. The man has her in his head.

The Wasps

The apples on the tree are full of wasps;
Red apples, racing like hearts. The summer pushes
Her tongue into the winter's throat.

But at six today, like rain, like the first drops,
The wasps came battering softly at the black glass.
They want the light, the cold is at their backs.

That morning last year when the light had been left on
The strange room terrified the heart in me,
I could not place myself, didn't know my own

Insect scribble: then saw the whole soft
Pelt of wasps, its underbelly, the long black pane
Yellow with visitants, it seethed, the glass sounded.

I bless my life: that so much wants in.

Musicians in the Underground

I was descending early, nobody around
And only the usual noises in the corridors which are
The tremor of departures and the wind
When the music started, there was no evading it
Wherever you might have been that morning underground

The wellspring was so deep and all the shafts and stairs
And the winding tiled runs were rinsed
On every level. How well they know
The acoustics of the system. That girl
Who stood in the rush hour at the mouth of one of the chambers

And showed ten thousand people the countenance of an angel
With closed eyes, singing. It was something
Not in our daily speech but still our language
Older, truer. Then how wrong
And slovenly my tongue felt. They visit the body and soul

Of every love and want and the night's lost dreams
They fetch them home. That boy, that faun
Who jumped us slumbering
And rode the lurching car and into the curves and down
The tunnels shivering under our clothes

We had him as conductor, his black horn
Lifted and moaning. These singers,
These couriers through the labyrinth out of the sight of the sun
They are as free as swallows and they know
What the ghosts felt once, and warn us while we can.

Angels

I know a few girls who might well be angels.
One with a passion for railways. Her most likely.
Show her a branch line vanishing in bluebells
She feels it like a thread. From here, she says,

Give me a week I'll be in Mozdok.
She has the connections at her fingertips.
I have a coward soul. I lie awake
Begging the saints and all the old gods

Whichever had responsibility for wayfarers
Watch her. Intervene on her side. Cancel
Oncoming human error. I see her
Stuck somewhere bad with no train out till Monday

Asking a bed for the night from total strangers.
Must be she wakes an ancient obligation:
This we should do, this we should never do
To strangers. She knows as well as anyone

What terminus the cattletrucks arrived at
But when she speaks of railways I imagine
Land black as space, the night trains
Seeding it through with conversations

To its starry points. Stories, stories.
People with nothing but the gift of tongues
Break that with her who leaves them when she chooses,
Fumble for something she will remember them by.

Angels are like that. Much as we do
They read the newspapers, they watch the news
But cast themselves on the wings of the world
The way not one of us does nowadays.

It is so easy to abuse an angel.
They show their open faces like the blind.
Be courteous. They expect it. That precisely
Is the gift of angels visiting our kind.

Poppies

Poppies have come up in last year's bean trenches.
Nobody tipped in any blood
All we did was back off a yard or so
The ground must be thick with their black roe.

There must be a desperate press under the roots
These two gashes are packed tight
There must be millions of poppies frantic for the light
Perhaps we shall give them another yard next year.

Poppies are what comes when we let the black earth sleep.
It seems they want the room we occupy.
Wake, and lifting the light blood in the lids
More and more poppies crowd against the eye.

The days come up bled white. They need the blood
Wrapped on a dot of black in every bud.
That colour waits in there like music in a score.
The tissue itches. The petals unclenching

Are harder on the cap than is a baby's head
On the tight vagina. So through scabs
And falling bits of scale life crowns.
Under the streaming sky it muscles out red.

Mistletoe

Holly is so robust, the mistletoe was
For kissing under, pale little drops,
I think she would bleed like that
She is so awash. I spend hours at the screen
Appealing, I have nightmares
That in the far north somewhere
On a coast swilled even now with fifty thousand tons of oil
There was a plant like the one the gods called *molu*
Or in a rainforest
Needle in a burned-out haystack the size of Wales
There was. When I implore the web
The word coming down to me most often is mistletoe.
A professor in Arizona bought his wife five years with it,
His beloved wife, and under the Pyrenees
A marvellous boy going white before their eyes
Is now as bright as holly. Day by day
I increase my stack of miracles
All certificated. I have given her the pearls
Necklace and earrings
And nailed a sprig on every lintel in our house.
Mistletoe was in Eden
Sucking the goodness out of Eve's own tree.

On Oxford Station, 15 February 1997

Then everything paused, it all went very quiet,
I watched a small cloud on the blue due north,
Blue that the iron tracks were levelled at,

Such blue, such quiet blue, it troubled me
Like something unimaginable that I could see
And didn't have the word for, I watched the cloud,

One white cloud on the quiet empty blue,
Light as a feather at the lips of life
Testing for breath, feeling for final proof.

Ground Elder

Once since he died I saw him in a dream
Wherever the dead are, he was jovial,
He clapped me hard between his hands and said:
Stay, but I would not and I came back here
Where the living are. Now it is April

And kneeling on the warm earth in a sort of shame,
Dumb, fearful, not fit company
For anything opening I begin again
Pulling the ground elder, its leaves
Show it like flags or floats, the hands go in

After it gently, where it breaks it lives
Like worms, every remnant sprouts, this is
The thing he told me it was like,
This work of crochet through the living ground,
This reproductive act without an end,

A little like, nothing is really like
It, only love perhaps, both strike
And spread. Gathering the long tubers,
Stupidly laying them out in an old bowl
As though they were edible helps, it eases

The grip, the dumbness. Anyone patient
Who kneels half a day in spring and labours
Works wonders here. The summer will live.
You never get it all out, as he said.
No matter here. Here it is different.

'We say the dead depart'

We say the dead depart but can't say where
And can't imagine being nowhere, time
Full-stopped. But absence
Is here and now, we rub along
Shoulder to shoulder with the vacancies
The dead have left, doing the best we can
Less well with poorer means and greater need
In a worsened world, to fill them. This week
Everyone sees the deficit, time running out
Everyone has the dead man's kindness in their view
Everyone needing it, no one
Meeting a friend of his this week
Has had an unkind word. And how alive
The world continues to be with things the dead man loved
Last week, goldfinches, say,
A charm, and how bereft they look, not so well admired, they want
Their due and look to us
The bereaved, his understudies.

Quaker Memorial Meeting

We are facing into a space
And watching roses on the table in a bowl
Dying so slowly it seems like stillness.

We are trying to concentrate. Outside
With the dead limbs buds are coming down
And blossom, weddings of it. Outside

The roses would be gone in a gasp, a heartbeat,
Shape and scent, but here under a roof
It is like the lying down time after giving blood

Or when the tide turns on anxiety and sleep comes,
The images arrive, like clouds
From somewhere inexhaustible, on a still blue sky

The white ghosts passing over. Sunlight blows
On and off and somebody stands
And speaks a memory of the dead man into the space

Or pool, the pool of our silences, and through
The haloes where the memory falls
In the collecting place like water writing

The images rise. In this, somebody says,
Like this he touched my life and since then
Less well, the best I can, I have been trying

To repay him to others, younger. Words
Like water flowers. My signature,
My wedded helix, will unravel in no time, soon.

But life rides on the winds. Love of the light
And creatures under the sun, the love
Like his that lifts our hearts now over the empty space

Is a love of the four winds. Into them
When we have fetched his shivering image to the surface
And remembered the shape he had and recollected

His qualities and the shape they took in deeds
We give him away and ourselves then also
Breaking up the meeting into the four winds.

Bonfires

Eight months dead, the sun low and silvery,
He was seen through the three bare apple trees
In that dirty mackintosh and crumpled hat

At the heap, near the ditch, feeding the fire.
It was himself, content. Now I will believe
There is after all an everlasting bonfire:

One in a sort of heaven. Like the animals
When they dive down very deep for the winter
A bonfire can retract to a small heart,

Keep warm, lie low, suffer the wind and the rain,
Hoarding a decision to come back to life.
The sign is a stiffening of its wisp of breath.

It hurries then, all the bulk, all the material,
Through cloudy white straits of smoke
It comes in a rush to the state of pure flame.

A scent of bonfire entered the house at elevenses,
Hung on his coat among the respectable coats
In the dark for days. Nobody wonders much

That he has been seen in the grey-green lichen light
Behind the trees we stripped this year without him
Making a smoke, bringing on a roar of flame.

Above West Shore, Llandudno

Their seats, before they come, are like
The empty sarcophagi in the Alyscamps
But named, named with the dead, in memory of,
Who loved this place, who often sat here,
Who loved the view from here

Over the red roofs of the homes
To the estuary, who loved the western sea,
Whose heart is here. Bad heart,
Bad in the chest, bad veins, bad bones,
These are the not-so-bads who haul themselves up here

By the handrail, often pausing, one step at a time,
For breath, up here
Where it is level and the many benches are
And the view is famous over the nursing homes
And hospices, to the estuary. They sit

Full in the sun with thyme, harebells,
And the open stars of carline thistles at their backs
And butterflies, the blues
That haunt the limestone, round their heads
And watch the estuary. Nice to go out like that.

There is no agony in the meeting of salt and sweet.
There is some give and take.
Observe how far upstream
The sea extends its life on a flood tide
And how the river lasts. Under the red roofs

Such indignities but here
Where the broompods crack and the gulls
And jackdaws keep on nattering and children
Shout all this way up from the lusty waves
The climbers sit in the airy light

With shades, with better halves
Continuing some talk and watch the waters –
That kind rocking, that cool fusion –
Glad that it was, wishing it had been,
Praying it will be as easy on them as that.

Soldiering On

We need another monument. Everywhere
Has Tommy Atkins with his head bowed down
For all his pals, the alphabetical dead,
And that is sweet and right and every year
We freshen the whited cenotaph with red

But no one seems to have thought of standing her
In all the parishes in bronze or stone
With bags, with heavy bags, with bags of spuds
And flour and tins of peas and clinging kids
Lending the bags their bit of extra weight –

Flat-chested little woman in a hat,
Thin as a rake, tough as old boots, with feet
That ache, ache, ache. I've read
He staggered into battle carrying sixty pounds
Of things for killing with. She looked after the pence,

She made ends meet, she had her ports of call
For things that keep body and soul together
Like sugar, tea, a loaf, spare ribs and lard,
And things the big ship brings that light the ends
Of years, like oranges. On maps of France

I've trailed him down the chalky roads to where
They end and her on the oldest A to Z
Down streets, thin as a wraith, year in, year out
Bidding the youngest put her best foot forward,
Lugging the rations past the war memorial.

Kaluga

Early, alone, before her teeth are in
She opens the morning paper and sees this:
A photo of a man in battledress
Masked so he has no nose or mouth or chin

But eyes, a surgeon's eyes, and bare
Hands. He tilts a skull
On his knee like a ventriloquist to pull
A living from it with pliers. And where

Do they dig like this? What foreign field? A place
She muddled up with Golgotha and said
Over and over when she went to bed

Aloud to nobody. She sees a face,
All of it suddenly, and a glimpse of gold
Top left, in 1940, when he smiled.

'Stuck fast'

Stuck fast, both eyes gone, not long dead –
Only a ewe in lamb, but I suppose
Whatever has a heartbeat and a head
Its terror is much the same. This seems devised

By one of those people (and there must be some)
Whose daydreams on the beach or driving home
Are `cruel and unusual punishments'
For if they get the chance – but isn't. Is

Mother Nature straight: a slit of mire
In which you fit exactly, the working feet
Nothing to purchase on, you know you are

Desperately visible, but only from the skies.
Nothing will come however loud you bleat
Except the thing that wants your bulging eyes.

'Eyeballs of quartz'

Eyeballs of quartz in the harsh conglomerates
The river rolls them back into the sea.
Up there a creature disarticulates
And tinkles downstream: pretty vertebrae,

A gushing skull, the white bars of the heart.
I fished a length out like a runner's baton
And climbed the waterfalls and found the start
And finish of the clues: a flooding basin,

In it a trap of stones, in that a shank
Caught by the foot, still feeling in the water,
And nothing else: the rest, the weight, the stink,
Was got cleanly away. The piece I brought there

Is fit to lay across the mouth. The remnant
Might wag for ever in its phantom torment.

Lamb

Hats off to the little chap
Eased out like a stool the colour of blood and mustard
On the edge above the sea
And the sea coming in with the wind the colour of steel and charcoal.

Sky like a slaughterhouse. We can't say much about him
But it must be a fact that the field is colder than the womb
And lying curled in there must have been easier
Than trying to stand in the wind on pipecleaners.

Perhaps to be terrified by a sky like this
You need some IQ and to have read the newspapers
And even this field —
Like a battlefield, afterbirths everywhere

And the crows we call the hoodies
The ones with capes of ash
Who are as inclined to mercy as a Kray or a Goeth
And will have your eyes and tongue out if you wander off —

Even a field like this and the corbies treading and tearing at the
        slung-around placentas
Perhaps it only upsets you if you've had an education. Still
The wind, and when I see night coming down
As warm and motherly as the God of Abraham and see him peering
        out

Through the wire at such a sea
Under a sky more like Cambodia's
Entrails in the jaws of Pol Pot
Than heaven, on his first night among us I say hats off to him.

Endangered Species

No wonder we love the whales. Do they not carry
Our warm blood below and we remember
Falling asleep in a feeling element
And our voices beating a musical way

To a larger kindred, around the world? Mostly
We wake too quickly, the sleep runs off our heads
And we are employed at once in the usual
Coveting and schemes. I was luckier today

And remembered leaving a house in the Dales
Like home for a night, the four under one roof,
I left them sleeping without a moon or stars
And followed my dreaming self along a road.

Daylight augmented in a fine rain.
I had the sensation of dawning on my face.
But for the animals (and they had gathered
The dark standing in fields and now appeared

Replete) the night dissolved, but in the light,
A grey-eyed light, under the draining hills
Some pools of woodland remained and in them owls
And beside my sleepwalking, along the borders

Owls accompanied me, they were echoing
From wood to wood, into the hesitant day
I carried the owls in their surviving wells
Of night-time. The fittest are a fatal breed.

They'd do without sleep if they possibly could
And meter it for the rest of us. I like
Humans who harbour the dark in their open
Eyes all day. They seem more kin, more kind. They are

The ones not listening while the ruling voices
Further impair our hearing. They are away
With the owls, they ride the dreaming hooting hills
Down, down, into an infinite pacific.

Warming

Signs and wonders. We carried an old man
To view his father in the ice.
He is visible in the costume of that day and age

Still ruddy
Like a strapping son. His boy would not come down again
But put on fur

And haunts him, gibbering. I went up higher.
I tell you there is no stillness any more
But groans, chutes and a noise like riddling.

Our little river meanwhile
Continues innocently in the usual voice
But we are remembering the accidents

And murders hereabouts. Who will be called
Each to his own
And lie face down on the clarifying ice

Over a wound in bloom?
At nights I listen to the little river
Prattling as though there were nothing more to say.

But think of the melt behind the teeth of the moraine
And look at the map: up fifty thousand valleys
Ice and gentians

Are ebbing away from us
To a sunny crown.
Has anywhere

For so much backing up
Widened the mouth enough to speak it
And the eyes to weep?

Athens

Dig where you like, you soon hit marble.
We slop our concrete over some wonderful things.
See where we cleared away to start again:
A temple of Aphrodite Ourania shows through.

Another hot night. Bullfrogs. Rats. The drains.

A citizen squats in a greenish light
Hawking videos, all dirty.
Many kinds of bug fall on his head
And a little old mother holds him by the ear for a chinwag.

Deeper, deeper
The electric rides us into the agora.

Master and Man

'Punto bläst Magnifique'

MOZART TO HIS FATHER,
(PARIS, 5 APRIL 1778)

1

Giovanni Punto, born Jan Václav Stich
At Tetschen, now Zehusice, in 1746,
Belonged to Wenzel Joseph, Graf von Thun,
But ran away when he was twenty to have a life of his own.

2

He was a hornplayer, the best in his day,
Best ever perhaps. Mozart wrote him K
297b, the *Sinfonia Concertante*, and Beethoven
The *Horn Sonata*, Opus 17.

3

Count Wenzel Joseph though was furious
For he had put money where Jan's mouth was,
Sent him to masters, the best, in Prague, Munich and Dresden
And wanted a long return on his investment.

4

Now he put money on Giovanni's head.
The ungrateful little swine is mine, he said,
What he produces is my property,
Every silver note. You bring him back to me

5

Or knock his front teeth out. Of this poor man,
Perhaps not one of the best of the von Thun clan
But who for all I know was kind to animals,
Feared God and listening to music in his soul's

6

Best part had once or twice been shown
Love, freedom, joy, nothing is known
Except his dates and in between the two
That thing he sent his bully-boys to do.

7

Easy to imagine Giovanni Punto
On a cloud in heaven playing the silver cor solo
Made for him in Paris by Joseph Raoux, the best,
And poor Graf Wenzel Joseph in distress

8

Sending to Father Abraham for one note
Of the waters of that horn to cool his throat,
Tongue, lips, and being told there is
Between a soul in torment and a soul in bliss

9

A great gulf fixed. I hope instead
He served his time in purgatory before he was dead –
At nights, dreaming it done, the worst, dreaming it carried out,
And woke, and wept for gratitude that it was not.

10

Wenzel was dead. Jan Václav Stich went home
King, through a multitude. His turn come,
He had himself sent off with Mozart's *Requiem*,
Mercy enough in it for both of them.

After the Opera

About now, the drunk time,
The house opens its sluices and the music leaves
Fast: the stalls and the raked circle,
The vertiginous faces of balcony

Hurry it off down the aisles and the back stairs
Into this city
Of boots, fists, smashes, sirens,
Every night about now.

There was another lazarus with a bandaged head
In a porky hat, lying on the back step,
When the children of paradise were tipped
Out of the gods, still singing,

And we all poured over him,
He was in the way, we might have stooped,
I suppose, and laid a coin on him
But nobody did, we might

Have pocked, spotted, armoured the man
With sheeny coins until he shone
Like King Fish, it would have done no good:
He needed notes –

Ours, our blood, our breath,
He needed the drunk, inhaled, ingested singing,
Which I suppose he heard through the iron door,
Sickly, coming and going,

Like the cricket in Australia
When a boy crept down in a safe and sleeping house
And lit the dial
And flattened his ear against the warming set

And the clapping heaved and broke. We clapped,
We made a thunder at his ear
And drained in haste like sudden torrential rain
To the level of the streets.

These few nights, always about this time,
A dose of happiness, of more
Than happiness, a sugar of faith,
A massive shot of love

Voids over him (for one) with the bloody face
At the heart of town
Among the sirens and the broken glass
And roars and fails and whimpers underground.

'Figures on the silver'

Figures on the silver, black;
Their game ending already.
I remember the game: the tide has to be just right.
Cognizance of the sands is also necessary.

Children and a dog. There should always be a dog.
He will not know the rules, he is the game's spirit,
Mad streaker through, mad circler of it.
He runs off the excess, or raises it.

The flat white island is so beautiful.
But the children are not there to be a spectacle,
They want the edge of the tide's exact sickle,
They can hardly wait, they beg the boundary

Come on, come on, come on.
The advance of pleasure over little ridges
And something in you somewhere sobbing make it stop,
Come on, come on. I remember that. It does

Come on, the runners have it warm around their ankles
Like skipping-ropes. The dog
Torpedoes them. This is the real game now:
Full tosses, slosh and slog,

Everything wet and sunny. They are bare shadows,
Substantial, quick, intensely black shadows,
Boys and girls cannot be told apart,
And all their vocables, rising this far,

Are only calls and cries. I should hate to be God
Or one among the dead watching from here.
How they must ache to give up the condition
And join the running on the water.

I know the game. How long will they play?
How deep? Stumps drawn
And floating with the bat, driftwood again.
The pitch is lidded under wrinkled steel.

The breathless dog has climbed this far, to me.
Perhaps I wished it, whistled him maybe,
Inclined myself, and felt his salty snout
Suddenly slobbering my drylander hand,

And the ball in it, the balding mangy ball,
The ball for the game, for more and more of the game.
He grins, he has Ben Gunn's demented eyes.
I scrumped you this from paradise, he says.

Kinder

That feather on the brow a mile away
Is water, the Downfall
Doing its uttermost to get over the edge
But hasn't the body and the wind erects it.

This is a queer place I have brought you.
More like a brain than acres of the open earth.
As complicated as a brain and spongey;
But black, all black. If water had volition

This dome would be its nightmare. The peat
Takes everything: false hopes, false starts,
Every crazy aberration. It rains,
The sky forgets, but where we are

The new arrival of water goes over them all again
And deeper. In the fogs
The thread you were following in these soft ravines
Ends. I never saw so many ends

Loose, sad, dead. Try climbing out –
Something's the matter with gravity
Or with your legs. Go in again,
Go deeper. Then nowhere, nowhere hopeful,

Suddenly you sense a slope, there is a downhill after all,
And you are setting right (how easily
Water can solve a labyrinth
That tilts) and you come clear and the lost tongue

Of water, the purling, the babbling,
Comes back to you and hungry for the edge, grateful,
The body strips – and hits up against that wind
And rises contrary to nature like a ghost

On view. My head is clear today.
I think I can lead you from the plume of water due east.
I seem to remember a cairn on the far edge.
There, in the lee, the water gets off headlong.

Bombscare

But we have bombscares. There was one this spring
The day before my birthday. I went in wanting
The OS map of another island
And sniffed the hush, the hush and a change in the air,
The two together: spring come and a bombscare.

A plastic tape was run all around the centre
Slight and symbolic as a sabbath wire
And nobody transgressed. The sentries
Had nothing much to do, but everyone expelled
From making a living in the centre idled

In shirt sleeves and blouses on the first day warm enough
With those kept out. You feel let off
Idling on the outside if you have to. Inside
It's like a site two thousand years from now
Uncovered clean. A police car like a UFO,

The blue light twirling. You feel absolved
More still when word comes out the thing was shelved
Among the goods a year ago at least.
The thought of it lying where you often came and went,
Its time not yet, is like a present

Coming from where you could not know one might. The tape
Ran to the shop but let me in. Sat on the step
In the sort of respite Sunday mornings used to make
Or overnight deep snow. Sat in the sun
And opened the map of another island there and then.

On the empty blue it floats like an elm-seed.
Seems mostly rock. The thin yellow road,
Run from a steamer route on the east coast,
Includes some tumuli, a standing stone or two,
A ruined oratory in the noose of its lasso.

Fifty tomorrow. From off the west coast
Peninsulas push out. The one pushing the farthest,
I fix on that. Sweet, sitting in the sun
While a man with nifty fingers whose job it is,
Breathing quietly, makes a timebomb harmless.

Don Giovanni and the Women

The notes are there, the dust is always there
And being sorted into arias
And shapes that answer to particular names

Again they feed his everlasting fire
And lapse into the cold with other flames
And cannot tell which ash was ever theirs

The ghostly women coming with a list
Who wanted naming like the glorious dead
They sift among the ashes and the notes

Their mouths are wide, they want his pulsing blood
Among the huddle every listed ghost
Wants her particular music in her throat.

Troubled by the airs of hell the dust assumes
More likenesses than anyone can bear.

A Meeting in the Library

Some good angel should have prevented this
But he is in love and all the angels are against him.
Chances, lots, coincidences
Fall in a way to hurt him, he is too much in love.
So looking up from reading about a courtly world,
Ordeals in hope, rewards for the brave, mercy,
He meets her eyes. Nothing is comparable,
Nothing so serious has been or will be again.
For in a moment of the purest ice
He sees what he cannot live his life without
Withheld. She is small, slight,
There is no blood on her lips, there are no serpents in her hair,
Her wrists are thin, her power is a terrible burden.

Then somebody tilts a window in that gallery
And the sun goes over the portraits of the poets
And the feeling tumbles into him again
After her lightning, and every writing in the library
Clamours to be uttered through his parted lips
And every line of writing has to do with hopeless love.
Nothing is worse, she knows it, she is a yard away,
They stand like statues between the banks of poetry
And for her the tongue in his mouth is a dead letter.

Llyn Conach

Sky bending over a water still hidden;
Track to the lip of it; familiar
Rising feelings; the eyes
Already wide for the moment of inrush. But then

The shock of this lake was peculiar
Like a crack through me. I saw
The ghost of myself passing from right to left
Along the rim, from those low hills

To that black plantation, anxious.
The gulls were clamouring and that tuft
Of an island and the couple of skiffs
Tethered and prancing on the agitated water were witnesses.

I can't date him exactly, couldn't tell you
How many times the skin of his hands has come and gone since then
But he was anxious, one summer evening, late,
Looking for somewhere to shut his eyes out of sight.

The wind is continuous, the serial
Of gulls runs on and on with the same clamour,
You would go into me twice, with a remainder,
But now we have come over the lip to this agitated water

Come closer in. I have the desire
To house you out of the wind under the slant roof
And within the walls of me. The wind
Is dressing your face in your sheer black hair

And I can't see until my hands go looking under. Then
Eastings and northings give a unique place
Time lights it once and you
You rush my heart, love, with the cold draught of a revenant.

Comfort Me with Apples

It makes me think of the men of the island of Pitan
Who lived off the scent of apples
And only that. Whenever they travelled
They took wild apples with them, to breathe in.

The sublimation of apples into pure savour,
The spirit of apple, the invisible apple platonic
Was all they ever wanted. Any vapour
Grosser than ghostly apple made them sick.

They were small men, Mandeville says, and had
No mouths. They lived on a river island in the East
Not far from Eden and the eye of God.

We can try, I suppose. It might not be easy
Doing without the flesh of apples and the waters of taste.
The mouth's the problem. Still, we can always try.

'You make the rules'

You make the rules. I rhyme ab ab
And think perhaps two tercets would be best.
They seem less final. So: cd cd
And efg repeated. For the rest

You say, I'll follow on. I scan the stuff
Ti-tum, ti-tum, ti-tum, ti-tum, ti-tum.
Getting the measure right's easy enough
And all the rest, the life of us, must come

To you to know what shape it should be in
And look like, feel like, do. Seems what we had
We haven't now and what we could we can't.

You are too soft for so much discipline.
Seems what seemed good not long since now seems bad.
Seems I must fit my baulked love how you want.

Sleep With

Can't even dream about you. The censors
Squat at the gates of horn and will not let you through
Until last night, incognita. I was sure it was you

And seeing you where you are not allowed to be
I supposed you had changed your mind and I ran headlong
To the one point again. Supposed wrong.

Behaviour is final in the underworld. They say:
I think I shall die of shame. And hear:
You can't, you have, and you will be ashamed for ever.

Sad. But listen. The next thing I knew
From that one point all my desires flew
Slowly, sweetly, they were sent away

Down routes of sleep, travelling to the ends of me
And nowhere touched on you more hungrily
Than your own sleep does and I was sure

This centrifugence suited you, for everywhere
We joined as easily as water, air or fire
And passed in give and take through truce to peace,

Levelling. I am sure it was you
And the way I lent myself to metamorphosis
Is like a gift I never knew I had. But now

The images that come to tell you how we met,
How light it was and how it played from head to toe
Like sunshine, like a warm sea fret,

All without panic, all without fear of doing any ill,
Seem disallowed, seem a touch gross, as though
My absence, finer and finer, would suit you better still.

'That place again'

That place again, the blank seawall,
The fact of the wall, like a wall of death, the sea
Slews off it at an angle calculable
And sickening, can't break, its energy

Gets swallowed back. In daylight, miles inland,
Still mulling over that dumb repetition,
This dawned on me as well: there was no wind,
Not a breath, not a whisper, and there was no moon,

Not a ghost, not a sliver, such unease
Wanting a mover, a sufficient cause,
A cold slant wind, a cold too-close full moon.

The sea in that place troubles me inland
Still heaving at it long after the last
Bright slip of her averted face was lost.

Cycladic Idols

In the night there were owls, so close
One on the chimney pot calling back
As though she had found me and were summoning the others.

The flat white face has visited again.
I warm my hands on coffee in a fired clay.
This bitter morning I am willing to listen.

Grow up, she says.
Your grown-up son was right not to sleep with me.
He has a healthy fear. Grow up yourself.

You will never see me in the flesh
Only in the bone.
Your eyes are incorrigible

As though a nipple in each would cool your migraine
Likewise your hands
Small and ugly and with bitten nails

As though one laid on my pubic bone would warm me through
Will they never learn? Again and again:
Where I belong is never warmer than moonlight

You had no right to fetch me in
I do not belong on your pillow
Your son was right to turn my face to the wall.

Owls are friendlier. I hug myself
For cold and nobody else
And nobody hugs me.

'All night the rain'

All night the rain and the little stream
Hurrying it away off the hill into other streams.
Why can't he sleep? Why can't the water be
For him a sweet accompaniment as it is for me?

And the wind, that I am warm and out of it
How this comforts my sleep and if I wake and listen
To the wind and the rain and the hurrying water
Sleep bides by me, I can turn to my sleep again.

His face in the morning, you would say
This hill and all the great hills east had been
His to run off the water from and the rain
Was him as well and he could only increase.

Why can he not rest? He says when first light came
He dreamed badly. Did I not hear him cry?
In nightmare he thought the wind was me and I
Had crossed the space and swung his hesitant door.

'The lakes, their stepping down'

The lakes, their stepping down
From one small lozenge of water
With skeeters on
And the wild horses come to the lip
With coats the colours of sedge.

I was higher still
Nearly asleep against the megalith
In a bluish mist
And heard the larks above it in the clear
Lifting the origin
Higher still.

From there
To here
Gift upon gift.

Cupping your hands like that reminded me.

'Mid-afternoon in another narrow bed'

Mid-afternoon in another narrow bed
High up in another thin hotel
Now they are watching swifts crossing the snow
And higher, higher, higher criss-crossing the blue.

Freed of their own they think the swifts' hunger
A love of life, and life all play,
All bodying forth some consummate ability
For the love of it, in freedom. Later when they go down

On the choking streets to seek a sharp red wine,
Succulent bitter olives, soft white bread
And oranges, and when they hear
The caged birds hung on balconies as though to test the air

Each in its shaft of sun
Singing as though to burst the heart and the cage
These two seeking their nourishment when they please
By that trapped singing will feel their hunger raised

Higher than the highest floor of their flung-up hotel,
Higher than the ravenous swifts, higher than the snow
Into the blue itself, the keen
Cold infinite and insatiable blue.

'Madame, you keep a good house'

Madame, you keep a good house. Tranquil? No.
The rock band seemed to be surging out of the toilet bowl
And between them and the bin men
Usually there's a drunk tossing bottles for the smash

Deep down. But we're not here for the tranquillity
It's the bed
That triples your stars in my book, the mirrors and the bed,
The mirrors, the white bed, the windows and all that sky. Night came

And the lightnings flicked and lifted on the south
And the morning with very slow silver aeroplanes
Cut up by swifts and the blue
And the cool sun came in on us. Mirrors are good

When you need to multiply to say the half of it.
Set them this morning
So we fuck to that point which must be near eternity
Where the light gives out, set them to broadcast

Multiple ghosts of us coupling over the rooftops. Madame
Bless you for the mirrors and for your balcony.
Now the deep street
Is as populous as the milky way.

I see the citizens feasting at the east end tonight
At trestle tables in the Place des Abbesses
Under a red moon. At the west
I know they are dust in their sepulchres tonight and every night.

Honey from Palaiochora

It is hard to make out where Palaiochora is
    From here. You have to look up, higher up
Than you'd ever think there could have been a town, and find
    The upright that is not a wavy cypress tree
And that's the tower, still standing, lifted like a minestack,
    A pale sign. The rest is above and below
On ledges but even after you've been up there,
    Even with the sun on it and though you find
The Venetian belfry that has stood through earthquakes,
    Still hard to believe from here. On the island
In spring being in or out of the sun is black and white:
    You huddle, out; but in you open up.

When we got down from finding Palaiochora,
    Carrying our heavy honey in a jar,
We made tea in a glass with a wheel of lemon in,
    Golden, and dug at the honey there and then,
Dripping it on broken bread with spoons. The sun rode down
    The line of the hill of Palaiochora
Full in on us. We slid the windows wide, we stripped,
    Every stitch off both of us, I took
The lingering honey and lemon off his tongue
    And had his hand and the sun together
Between my legs, idling, the way I wanted it,
    Slowly, slowly, so that they gave me time

For all the roofless houses of Palaiochora,
    Gone in now under the lee of the sun, back
Into the hill with all their clever paths and steps,
    To appear behind my eyes: flowers, flowers,
White irises and asphodel, poppies and drifts
    And flounces of purple vetch where people slept
And where they cooked and talked and over their wells and walls
    From level to level through their workplaces,
Terrace into terrace ushering through flowers and
    Everyone long since gone, centuries gone,
Except in the unroofed chapels under the sun
    Where it came and went and they were warm or cold

Only the fresco angels, they had stayed, they looked
    Ghostly in the day, ghostly in the flowers,
Being made for the dark and to come out glowing
    Under a roof with candles and now revealed
And fading day by day in the visiting sun:
    Angels blessing, angels announcing, but with
Faces of the boy or girl you would wish to have,
    Earthly, pleased, lifted, and showing a pale palm
For a sign where we found them, tall as adolescents,
    In the irises and the purple. Then I
Was in shadow, his, his hot shade, and felt for the sun
    Down the line of his back and as though he were

The sun I pulled him in, in, to ensure in me
    Before the lingering angels faded
Some seed of the flowers of Palaiochora
    Heaped in the standing frames of empty homes
Like quilts and linen, to have them body and soul
    Before the message and the blessing failed
In me while he was doubled by the sun I widened
    Where he reached and gave and met. Then waking,
Opening real eyes on a room replete with sun,
    Sun held on us above black cypress candles,
I saw our jar of honey. It was lit from in,
    From in itself. I saw that first. It shone.

LADY HAMILTON
AND THE ELEPHANT MAN

*Verse for four voices
with a prologue*

NOTE

Emma Hamilton and Joseph Merrick, a hundred years apart, were famous in their generations, she for her beauty, he for his sad deformity. Emma, born to poor parents in Cheshire in 1765, exploited her assets the best she could; and after standing as the Goddess of Health at the Adelphi to advertise a dubious medical practice she passed from Sir Harry Featherstonhaugh (by whom she had a child) to the Honourable Charles Greville and from him, in 1786, to his uncle, Sir William Hamilton, widower, Ambassador in Naples and passionate amateur of classical art and Mount Vesuvius. She seems really to have loved Greville and to have resented being passed on; but, with her mother, she made the best of it, established herself in Naples, got Hamilton to marry her, had a liaison (and another child) with Lord Nelson, the Hero of the Nile. With Hamilton as her impressario she entertained many guests in his household by 'standing in attitudes' – that is, by impersonating famous characters in ancient history and mythology. Many artists depicted her.

Joseph Merrick, born in Leicester in 1862, began to develop his deformity in infancy, but managed tolerably well at home until his mother died, when he was ten. His life thereafter worsened as his illness did, and he had to make shift first as a door-to-door salesman then in the workhouse. He escaped that misery by exploiting his one asset, his deformity, and put himself on the road, with a manager, as the Elephant Man. Being shown in a shop opposite the London Hospital he was visited by the surgeon Frederick Treves. Treves took him up, exhibited him at the Pathological Society, published articles on him. After an unhappy time on the continent Merrick came back into Treves's care in the London Hospital and lived out the remaining four years of his life there. Ridiculously, it was rumoured he might be Jack the Ripper. He was much visited by ladies of the highest society. The most recent medical opinion is that he suffered from Proteus syndrome.

Those are the bare facts on which I have based my poem. I have brought the four characters together in an underworld where they can converse and utter things it would be harder to utter in the prosaic daylight. The poem works through its images which connect and re-connect, as themes and suggestions in music might. Emma Hamilton, standing in attitudes, kept silent; Joseph Merrick had an inner life which his deformed mouth could not articulate. I wanted to let them speak, and their minders too. The symmetry attracted me, and the likenesses and differences it contained.

PROLOGUE

Said to be windy like the underground and crowded
Fuller than the undergrounds of London, Paris,
New York, Tokyo, Mexico City,
Fuller than the sum of all our cities in the rush hour, in one
Everlasting rush hour, is the underworld
The dead go down to, finishing. Trains arrive,
Emptying thousands through the corridors and out of the air we
      breathe
Steeply down come the moving stairways, thousands
Step after step the floor of the underworld
Creams off and the iron steps,
Clicking like tellers, wrap and go back for more. Listen where you will
Under the bare sky of a city park or in the precinct under a coloured
      dome,
By any entrance, by any of the thousand staircases in every city
What you will hear over the clicking plates and through
The moans of trains and through the wind
Or in the wind, for ever blowing down the wind,
What you can hear are voices, nervous tongues,
All the world's tongues being talked at once, a slithering noise
Like ice or broken glass, like dead leaves in the throat
And a harsh frost on the tongue. I would call it a whispering
But this is as loud as they can, the tongues of the whole wide world
At once, when you listen at a vent or where the stairs go down
Are only as loud as this whispering though they strain
However hard and are as plentiful as dots of dust. Listen,
Listen as hard as they are straining to be heard. Hear how the
      after–life
Prolongs them a while. What you can hear
Rushing through the dry throats, wagging the dry tongues,
These are the thoughts, the unsaid thoughts,
The never enough said thoughts, like spores
Leaving them now in millions, their thoughts and dreams
And everything never realised in a rush
Now leaving them as fast as they can exhale. But an average life
Will take a thousand years to end, it may be a thousand years
Before a soul has emptied, there is so much to tell,
Every little average life will whisper a thousand years
Before the soul is quiet.

Think of them crowding down the escalators
Arriving every minute on the crowded trains
Uttering all in a rush the things that wanted saying.

The harsh dry whispering gets louder. It sounds like cicadas in the south or roosting starlings in the north. Then it clarifies into the babble and din of city streets, Naples in the 1780s, London in the 1880s, so that both English and Italian street cries may be heard.

SCENE ONE

Emma Hamilton and Joseph Merrick. She is pushing him in the wheelchair he used more and more in the last months of his life. The noise of street cries subsides into an undifferentiated whispering. Out of this then surfaces first Joseph's then Emma's voice.

JOSEPH: This whispering, this whistling
It was always so
My tubes and my flutey voice
The breath and the words
Never quite getting through
But never silence
Always a racket in my head and in my chest
An itchy noise
Like starlings
Much like here
Much like the starlings over Bedstead Square
The way they came on us in the foggy season
The short days shortening
Above our sooty brickwork the fiery days
Ending red as a cut throat
In came the starlings
Down on us
As many starlings
As there are cells in a body of suffering
And black as the devil's wing
The itch, the rattle
Much like that
The hospital
The streets
In me and outside me
Always this whispering.

60

EMMA: Me, I was told to hush
   And look nice. I spoke common, you see,
   A barbarous vernacular.
   That's why they taught me Italian
   And gave me singing lessons.
   Warbling Italian I did very nicely
   But otherwise
   Sir Willum sat in the front row with his finger on his lips
   And wanted attitudes
   And the mouth shut
   Or if I opened it – for the passion, you know –
   Then nothing coming out.

JOSEPH: Always open, mine
   On account of the stump of my trunk
   And sideways, as though to say something sarcastic
   Which I never did. I emitted a fluting sound
   As high as the voice of a principal boy
   And unintelligible except to Mr Treves
   A continuous whistling
   My soul being very voluble
   And life so short and the waking hours
   In educated company so few. All my courting
   The verbal at least
   Was done through Mr Treves.
   He englished me to the lady
   Not always faithfully.
   I had to listen while he toned me down
   And some days
   Knowing he would, trusting him to,
   I let rip from the depths.
   He made me palatable
   And never chided me afterwards. Truth is,
   In the case of Mrs Auberon
   I believe he would have said the same himself
   Only for the laws and decencies
   I believe he envied me my silver tongue
   And even the depths
   I really believe some days sitting between us
   In tight clothes transmitting
   Me to her
   He envied me my depths.

EMMA: Yes, in bed
    He didn't mind it rough
    The tongue, my bedtalk
    Rough as a cat's
    But mostly what he liked was looking.
    The way they look!
    True, I was special
    But all the same
    Turning me this way and that
    Hours at a time
    Eyes like something very hungry
    And his long nose
    And not quite smiling mouth
    Looking and looking
    As though he had nothing else to do
    And him an ambassador
    With a king to serve.
    You wouldn't believe it to see me now
    This weight of flesh
    The penury and the gin.
    If God were a gentleman
    He'd let a lady come to Hell as she was in her prime.
    Oh, I was sweet then!
    Only look at my pictures.
    I was a treasure then.
    You wouldn't think it to see me now.

JOSEPH: Myself, after infancy
    I was never a pretty sight.
    They pruned me but it grew again.
    And yet my mother was beautiful.
    I pitied her:
    A limping child
    Deforming under her very eyes.
    A mercy she never lived to see the worst.
    Stepmother put me out
    As anyone would.
    I was an extra mouth
    And such a mouth.
    I tried selling matches
    But the housewives shut the door in my swelling face.
    It occurred to me in the workhouse
    That the gross deformities of my osseous and cutaneous systems

Were all the stock I had.
I wrote an advertisement and got a promoter.
And you?

EMMA: The same.
There's not much of a living in female virtue
But lips like mine, a melting eye
And all the rest
There's a living in them if you can get a protector.
I stood at the Adelphi
In the Temple of Asclepius
Lightly veiled
For Doctor Graham
To show the public what his herbal baths could do.
Gents with gout
Had a good peer at me
Sweet sixteen
Nearly.

JOSEPH: I was on the road after that
With the wild animals and Nature's novelties
Scaly Boy
The Merino Girl
Flipper
Mrs Lip
And Mademoiselle Electra, the Electric Lady.
Among them I was not very extraordinary
And when I consider the handbill
Showing me perfect elephant from the neck up
I wonder the public didn't shout for their money back.
I was a poor display
Not funny
The smell of me for one thing
An exceedingly foul odour, according to Mr Treves
Not beastly
Not the brute beast in the warm stink of health
But rotting.
I have read there is a tree like that
Smelling as I did, in its fruit
A rotting weight.
How I loved the real elephants
Though one parading through Leicester knocked against Mother
When she was carrying me

And I came out with a tendency that way
A yearning
Never completed.
But I was on the road in my private caravan
And with the boss
Always went fifty–fifty.
How about you?

EMMA: I got a lord
As they said I'd be bound to with attributes like mine
I was soon snapped up.
He was rich and dim
With no proper mouth, it sort of slid away
But I came a cropper despite Mother's advice
And he put me out
As anyone would
Who couldn't be certain he had fathered it.
Mother gave me an earful:
We were doing well, she said
And now the mire.
But God was good
And Mother did some canvassing
And the Honourable Charles Greville took me on
With child
And Mother
And established us in his little house on the Edgware Road
The only condition being strict virtue:
Never to look another pair of trousers in the face.
I signed toot sweet
And Mother bought a new hat.
Whorehouse otherwise
Worked to death.

JOSEPH: Workhouse otherwise.
I was happy with Mr Norman and the elephants.
He wore white gloves
And called himself the Silver King.
He showed me on the Whitechapel Road
In a greengrocer's opposite the hospital
And there Mr Treves came for a private view
And was so smitten
He desired me for Science
And had me across the road without delay

In front of a camera
Naked as Adam, this way and that.
The bum, the *déhanchement*,
My private parts
Which being unafflicted seemed of unusual beauty
He pointed me all out
To students and fellows of the Royal Pathological Society
And measured me
And wrote me up for a publication
Then back to the Silver King in the greengrocer's
Where, to be honest, I was happier
Keeping my loincloth on.
I was saving for an early retirement.
I had set my heart on a disused lighthouse
With all the classics round the walls in nice editions
And old friends visiting.
Meanwhile we worked my sorry assets
Here and there
Wherever we could get a premises
But times change
And what I was aiming at eluded me
For with the progress of civilisation
The constables arrived to close the show
In the name of public decency
And I passed to an Italian
Who said he would try me on the continentals
But I went down badly
For by then I was more frightening than enlightening
And he dumped me in Brussels
With just enough for the steamer.
Imagine that.
But you?

EMMA: And you without the language
And nothing to recommend you to the passers-by
The way a girl does
Looking up from under her bonnet.

JOSEPH: I wore my famous cloak
And cap and veil.
The urchins lifted it
And when they saw my snout
And the drivel of my mouth
Which was all the speech I could manage in their tongue

They fastened on me
Dogs on a badger
And I backed towards the ports
Saying to myself: In my native land
Pretty far north
There is a parish whose responsibility I am
And a workhouse in which, when I am weak enough,
They will let me die in peace among the incurables.
That was the height of my aspiration
As I shifted like a crab someone has trodden on
Towards a boat. But you?

EMMA: Mother said: Em, this will do very nicely
Mr Greville seems to be a gentleman
Only keep your nose clean.
So I did. Sir Willum called.
He had come home to sell his vases and bury his wife.
On my white arm his sunburned hand
Looked like a blackamoor's.
He was lean and fit from climbing Vesuvius
Sixty-three times already
And never wearied.
He loved old pots and cinders
And me. He took me on his lap
He called me the fair teamaker of the Edgware Road
And said if ever... But my heart belonged to the nephew
The Honourable Charles Greville
And the uncle was fifty-four. We were doing very nicely.
Then one fine day he packs us off to Naples
Mother and me
For a holiday, he said, and to improve my colour
And that was that.
He passed me on like an antique pot
To the old devil, his uncle
The collector. And you?

JOSEPH: To Mr Treves? An intervention of Almighty God.
Picture me collapsed in the public waiting room
On Liverpool Street Station
And nothing coming out from under my cloak
To enlighten the mob
But the snivel and smell of fear.
Or don't.

No lady should have to.
I imagine you slim and perfumed and your skin
As soft as the softly lathering water of the north country
And as beautiful unclothed as the girl riding ashore
On a scallop out of the foam
And will not have you dwell on what I was like under my cloak
But a constable put in his hand at the slit
And found my good left hand
Soft as a girl's, soft as your own perhaps
And in it the card I had from Mr Treves
For if ever I wanted to come in under his wing.
He arrived like the God of Healing in a hansom cab
And took me into heaven
Which was a cellar room in Bedstead Square.

The voices fade into a whispering.

SCENE TWO

Sir Frederick Treves and Sir William Hamilton, strolling.

TREVES: 1886, the 24th of June
He was worse, in the eighteen months
Since my first photographs
Yet more exuberant
Were the papillomatous growths
Dusky purple
Deeply fissured
In more districts
And fouler, and the exosteses on the skull
The size of tangerines when I last saw him
Jaffas now.
Besides that he was chesty and under the bulk
His spine was buckling and his heart was overburdened.
I gave him four years
Correctly. The stench
Made one yearn for a clean cremation
But baths morning and evening reduced it.
I did the measurements again
And a few more plates
To record the stations of his agony.

HAMILTON: The 26th of April 1786
    She arrived in my house like Persephone
    Except not virgin
    But in the full of spring.
    She was twenty-one that very day.
    She called me Sir Willum
    Or Uncle Pliny
    And how to get her to view me otherwise
    Exercised me cruelly.
    My nephew Charles
    Cold as a flatfish
    Commended her to me as a cleanly bedfellow.
    She was, he said,
    The only woman he had ever slept with
    Without offence to one or other of his senses.

TREVES: He slept propped up for fear
    Of tolling backwards
    Headlong, headfirst down the pit of his nightmares
    Fast as a gannet
    Smack into death.
    Curious to watch him sleeping in the greenish light, the head
    Like one of those creatures we should never have known
    But for the microscope. He breathed
    As though through swamp.
    His hands lay on the counterpane side by side.
    Often they touched
    Often they even interlocked
    And they were the signal of his hope left out all night
    Outside his sleep
    More than companionable, the one
    Like a slip of a girl
    Friends with the bloat
    Poor other
    Night after night, the good one unafraid
    Doing her best to give the beast her virtue.

HAMILTON: In the eighteen months or so
    Since she made tea for me at his house on the Edgware Road
    She had put on a little.
    I saw we had no time to lose
    And called in artists immediately
    To fix her at her best

On the lip of going over
Into weight and the blurring of the fine line.
As a resurrection of the nymphs on vases
Or the goddess Flora from Herculaneum
My Emma at twenty-one
Was, to be frank,
Already at the limits of suitability
But in my leanness
I felt I had the world's best appetite
For softness such as hers
Almost a right to it
As any man may have to his particular vice.

TREVES: For two hours every Sunday
I absented myself from the cleanliness of my wife and children
For him
To learn his language
Expecting nothing
And learning it only as one might some barbarous dialect
For Science
But when I understood
I found he had the literature of a civilised man
And the dreams of a lovesick boy.
I heard the heart of the man
Overflow out of the left side of his mouth.
I thought I was inured to suffering
Other people's
After years in the East End
But this touched me: he had a mind
In the hideous cavern of his head
And a soul
Beating, beating like a trapped angel
Deep among his growths
And news of his life underground
Came up for my hearing on the waters of his mouth.

HAMILTON: Indeed? I was there at Pompeii
At the Temple of Isis
When they dug Polyhymnia
The Muse of Mime
Out of the ash. She has her finger laid across her lips
For silence. My Emma sat for hours
Thinking her thoughts, I suppose,
For painters, sculptors, workers in clay and bronze,

69

Ivory, enamel and all the precious stones
And stood for me
In diaphanous dresses
Tailored after the dresses of the dancers
Who under sixty feet of ash at Herculaneum
All that time were there. Our coffin-maker
Did me a frame of ebony
To stand her in
On a drop as black as the long night of the buried cities
And bring her forth
As warm as flame
And in the cool chiton
In the attitude appropriate
She was every passionate woman of the Ancient World
Before my audiences
I stood with a torch as they do in the galleries
When you visit at night and in the flicker
The statues seem to move
And as my Emma froze
I showed as much of her as it pleased me to
Always mute
Evening after evening, a serial
Through history and the legends
And in the nights
Once she had seen the way things had to be
And negociated dutifully for the upkeep of her mother
And care of the infant fostered in Lancashire
And got the necessary promises with regard to herself
As was proper
Then in my nights
Being shown the vases I do not usually display
Studiously she did her imitations.

TREVES: And the inner life?

HAMILTON: I liked things as they were
And the better the more their selves were on the surface.
See the lines on a red-figure vase:
Nothing is thwarted, nothing is down below
Still choked and begging for utterance.
All that muck about the inner life.
The sun is best
And how things look in it.
And when she fattened still I indulged myself

I gorged on her as long as possible
Afterwards clearing my head with vases
And the image in carnelian
Of how she was
And with the mountain
And its abundant clinker
Intolerant of human life.

TREVES: Off Lulworth once yachting
I got becalmed and for a while did nothing
To stop the drift. At that time –
It was before my science failed to save my daughter –
There was nothing the matter with my life,
No unusual grief.
I had domestic love
And power in my profession.
The case of Merrick occupied my mind
And for his favourite visitor
The young and pretty widow Mrs Auberon
I nourished a secret passion
Innocently enough. I mean to indicate
That I had, as we say,
Everything to live for, but off Lulworth
Letting it drift
I lay back on an element hostile to human life
Fagged as an old man
And the horror of London crept over me
Across the sweet haymaking shires
Across the quiet blue water
The deep filth of the East End came over me
As never when I was up to my elbows in it
Cutting, swabbing, stitching.
Understand me aright:
This was not the hopelessness
Every physician feels from time to time
Against such odds
But a marked advance of contempt.
We are a poor lot after all
And how clean the sea is
And better if London were under it
And nothing breathing in a human way.
I had a strong inclination
To go out with the tide

Somewhere clean
Vast
And immeasurably indifferent.

HAMILTON: Just so. Up there
Often my interest inebriated me
And I stood in a mad hilarity
Like cannon-fever
Bareheaded under a rain of pumice
And let the larger rocks
Every one a man-crusher
Land where they liked.
The mountain tanned my hide
And had this place we have come to now been fiery
I should have been quite at home.
When I conducted their Majesties
And all the court
To the great flow of 1771
How I despised them.
Nobody loved the mountain to my satisfaction
Except Bartolomeo
My first and only guide
A savage
Whose proper name was Cyclops.
He taught me the trick of walking on the moving lava
On its crust
And the love of the pretty crepitations
The magma makes advancing
I had from him
A monosyllabic man in one language.
We spitted turtle doves
And toasted them on the liquid fire
And a bottle of Lacrimae Christi
Went to and fro from mouth to mouth
Unwiped. I liked his company
And my own better still
High up on the rim
Or pottering for hours over the slag heaps.
You would not believe how colourful cinders are
All the ochres and umbers
Every degree of red
And black, such perfect black.
Then why did I come down

Among the imbeciles?
For red–figure vases
Their cool fine lines
And the luxury of Emma
So soft after the clinker.

TREVES: I've opened royalty
And Whitechapel whores
And must admit their innards are much the same.
I never used a knife in anger
And probably did more good than harm.
My early coat
Had been so stiffened by the blood and dirt of the work
It stood up without me.
I have bequeathed it to the College Museum
To stand among their curiosities
The tiny Paget woman bent like a bracket
The giant
The twins
And Merrick himself
Whose spine was like the snake of Asclepius.
I hope they will represent me next to him
In the carapace of my bloody coat.
As you came down off the mountain
So I came in again off the salt water
And crossed the meadows and the downs
To the Whitechapel Road
Where the whores in fights
Dug one another's faces out with broken gin bottles
And the Ripper ripped them.

SCENE THREE

Joseph, Emma, Treves, Hamilton, strolling, the last three taking it in turns to push Joseph in his wheelchair. Their speeches, though uttered aloud, are more like inner voices and are connected with one another only casually.

EMMA: The devil, that September
Before I had made my mind up
And was still pining after the other devil
The nephew

73

The uncle took me to see the whores
Me and Mother
Pretending the coachman missed the way
We got in among those streets
And he watched my face
When we saw the women and the girls in their windows and
        their doorways
Some without noses
Some with cuts
And the worst were the pretty ones
As soft and pretty as me
Already knowing what they would get to look like.
He was watching my face
And I almost said aloud:
Don't worry, I take your meaning, Sir Willum
And that night Mother said:
Did you take his meaning, child?
Poor Sir Willum
By that time I could have hooked the King himself
With my little finger
But I said to Mother: Don't worry, Mother
I'll make him marry me.

JOSEPH: Had you done as I asked
    And procured me a blind girl
    When all I wanted was to look at her
    The Fund would have stretched that far
    And all I wanted was to see her in the firelight
    In a romantic privacy such as bachelors enjoy
    There would have been no harm in it
    For the hour while she stood before me
    Or sat in my special armchair
    And we had some conversation while I looked at her
    And my good hand and the smell of my pommade
    Would have assured her she was with a gentleman
    Eccentric but a gentleman
    She would have touched on nothing abnormal
    And gone away richer by whatever the Fund allowed
    Had you done as I begged you to
    Instead of driving me to surface from my den
    On the worst nights in my cap and cloak and veil
    And trail those hellish streets where the very thought of me
    Blanched the women in their black doorways.

74

TREVES: In further, in deep
　　His genitalia hid like Sleeping Beauty
　　Awake, aware the circumambient
　　Stuff was changing. She slept
　　And never felt the light
　　Thicken and set in an unheard of way
　　And if she dreamed it as a darkening in the skull
　　There was an exit when she opened her eyes again
　　And a deliverer
　　And she resumed where she left off, barely begun,
　　Only just opening and not one drachm
　　Of flesh put on and not a single minute's extra weight, but he
　　I suppose him fled up in the fork of him
　　Far in as he could get
　　And there watching. The arm was as conspicuous
　　As the youngest brother's wing
　　Left out when all the rest returned
　　Into human shape and that is where
　　I advised his visitors to begin and keep their eyes on that
　　His perfect hand and arm and to only one
　　To her behind the mourning veil
　　Did I ever confess that other little remnant:
　　The penis and scrotum hiding unconverted.

HAMILTON: One curious thing:
　　We were digging a pleasure house on the east side of the city.
　　We found the phallus on the door
　　And pictures of the positions round the walls
　　For clients to point at who had no Latin
　　And the prices. Amusing
　　But I wanted more.
　　Ashed in the cellar there were skeletons
　　Some jewellery, a shoe
　　But I wanted more
　　And sent the men away for their siesta.
　　In that heat
　　Sweating like a convict
　　Breaking my fingernails
　　I got out the mask of one of the girls
　　Her real face
　　Mudpacked, and more
　　The imprint of a breast
　　Cupped perfectly and able to be purloined.

That was a year or so
Before I felt her heartbeat under my hand.

EMMA: I forgot who I was sometimes
Standing there
Being done
And whoever was doing me had to remind me.
Look homeward, he said,
Seeking the land of the Greeks with heart and soul
Or think of England. I did:
Mudflats, the fog
And folk like crabs. By then
England had sunk like one of her grey puddings
And I was nicely where I was.

JOSEPH: That autumn: Kate, Long Liz,
Dark Annie, Fair Emma
And Polly Nichols on our very doorstep.
I came up most nights and stood at the railings
In the yellow fog.
I will be forgiven for liking a fog
The yellower the better
The way it snuggled around the lamps
I could stand for hours
Watching the nurses
Angels of mercy
Passing overhead on the lighted walkways
From duty safely to their single beds
Above the streets
That worked into the body of the hospital
Or say we pushed
Into those sleepless streets
The respite of our wards and garden
Pushed, pushed
And I stood at the head of that endeavour
Gripping the railings
The fountain flopping at my back.
I was never cold
In the small self under my vast apparel
And at a certain hour I fitted my skeleton key
And exited
And slouched along the sweating walls.

76

TREVES: Animal, vegetable or mineral. Some mornings
He seemed more tree than elephant.
He reminded me of a weeping ash in my Dorset garden
That had collected swellings. At another hour
He resembled a waxy stalagmite
That puts on weight and sweats.
It is not long since we believed in the vegetation of stones.
Eminent men who had been underground
Told us the wet was the wet of generation
And the walls, the floor, the ceiling were heaving in the act
Only too slowly for our kind of vision.
Not long ago this was our explanation
Of one phenomenon among the millions
That prowl the rim and show their snouts and eyes
At night in the little firelight of the mind.

HAMILTON: Of the dead at Rosano
Calabria
In the terrible earthquake of 1783
The males were found in attitudes of struggle
But the female attitude
Was one of resignation. Yes,
They covered their heads and lay still
Unless they had children with them
And then they were found
In attitudes protective of the children.
I enquired particularly after this distinction
And found it everywhere confirmed
In all the flattened towns.
And a girl was recovered after eleven days
Holding her baby close
Who had died after four
And a woman went out on the tidal wave
Ark on the flood
And landed in labour
Safe.

EMMA: And then Medea
Who butchered her kiddies.
I was never much of a mother
But nor was Mother.
I did the Virgin once
Rolling up my eyes
But only for sport

To amuse Sir Willum in a church we were visiting.
The reverend father never recovered, I believe.
Sir Willum's favourite was Circe.
That always went down well
The old magic
Show 'em an ankle
Give 'em a look up an open sleeve
They moon
They pinken
You hear like a squeaking where they keep their tongues
Oink oink
Watch their trotters.
Sir Willum liked to observe me
Metamorphosing his gentlemen.

JOSEPH: Polly, the first girl,
Soon after the real thing
She was done in wax the way they found her
And shown where the Silver King showed me
In the back room of the greengrocer's
Opposite the hospital
Only a hundred yards from Buck's Row
Which was the place itself.
It preys on your mind a thing like that.
I mean:
Working in wax is a skilled job.
If I'd had two good hands
And the Guardians would have allowed it
I'd have modelled a lady after my heart's desire
Brought her forth
Out of the den of my head
Out of the cyst of my heart
And set her before me for some conversation
Had I had two good hands
And wax or clay
And the Guardians had allowed it.
Make, mend, rip:
What can a man not do with a good pair of hands?

TREVES: My colleague Openshaw
Received a ginny kidney
From Hell, as the letter said.
Or half, to be precise, the other half
The man had fried and eaten. In those days

I sat with Merrick oftener than I should have done
On Sundays after communion
But also in the afternoons
Oftener than I should have in the afternoons.
I was contented in his underground apartment
Like a badger's sett
In Bedstead Square.
Neither the crying on the streets
Nor the crying on the wards
Got in down there. We had it cosy
Lamplight and firelight
And always hoped Mrs Auberon would arrive.
I remember the feel of cold
And the scent of fog in her clothing.
She was cheerfulness itself
And I interpreted to her
From Merrick's mouth.
I say we were cosy
(She might bring things for tea)
But when she put back her veil
And showed all the beauty of her face to Merrick's one good eye
And took his delicate girlish hand in hers
And I conducted what came up in him
To her
His love and praise
I felt I was present at things I do not believe in
Fables, the myths
Present in my civil clothes by a dispensation
Because they needed an interpreter
Present and apart
As the lady I had chosen for her fortitude
Because no other could look at him and live
Inclined her visage over him
Nearer and nearer his erupted surfaces
As though by an emanation of her beauty
To translate him.
The heart of myth is horror
And coming up
Among the dripping asters in the garden
And showing her out like a clandestine affair
To a hansom waiting at the iron gate
I heard the crying on the wards again
And sniffed the streets

The black night thickening the yellow fog
That autumn
Which was the autumn of the Ripper's rushed postmortems.

HAMILTON: Everything is curious
More or less
And nothing matters. But when I remember
One winter how a cape of snow
Was wrapped around my beloved mountain's shoulders
And the lava trickled down it scarlet
And when I picture Emma before she fattened
Advancing with an arm outstretched
In prohibition or command
As a girlish Circe
And I remember doing caesareans on chamber tombs
And lifting pots from the grasp of skeletons
Or my mouth thinks
Of strong cheese on my picnics with the Cyclops
And wine
The mountain's wine
Then I pray this bloodless limbo wil not last much longer.
Palate and hands
And the eyes
Perhaps especially the eyes
So many years in a classical sun
Cramming the eyeholes with phenomena
My senses have enjoyed too much
And against their ghostly afterlife
Their want of blood
I want complete extinction.

EMMA: With only the one body
(Though that exceptional)
And a few shawls and maybe a wand
Or a Grecian urn
My job was to be all the females possible
So multiplying
His sole possession.
I understood this perfectly well
Not being as stupid as they thought I was.
In an average show
I might be a dozen doers and sufferers of terrible things
With beautiful difficult names

And the trick was
To pass from one to the next in a wave
So you were always becoming something and going over
Into something else. Mr Walpole called me
Sir Willum's gallery of statues
But it was better than that
Because I was warm and moved
Quick as water and the sunshine on things
More like dance
But with the little moments of being still
So that the gentlemen thought they had a statue
Or a figure on a pot
For a brief time
And then I was off and they couldn't seize me.
One show we practised and practised but never put it on.
I was to go through twenty metamorphoses
Of women into the inhuman:
Daphne into the tree
Io into the cow
Niobe into the stone
And ravished Philomela with her tongue cut out
Into the nightingale.
That sort of thing.
Sir Willum had twenty lined up in a sequence.
I did my best
But he asked too much
I was fullish by then
And Philomela for example was a chit of girl
So he went back to looking at his pots
And I did him Messalina
With one fair hand.

SCENE FOUR

Emma and Sir William, arm in arm.

EMMA: Again, Sir Willum.

HAMILTON: Must we, my darling?

EMMA: It passes the time. There is so much time.

HAMILTON: Running out, I trust.

Listen to the slithering sound of the sands of our lives
Dead grains
Running out
With a sound like the cicadas
In the dry heat I loved.

EMMA: Then be quick. Remember again.
Keep the memories alive.

HAMILTON: I want them dead
The sooner the better.

EMMA: I want them alive
As long as we can
Please, Sir Willum.

HAMILTON: Very well, my love.
You begin.

EMMA: Me as the Seamstress, by Mr Romney.

HAMILTON: Ditto, a Bacchante, by ditto.

EMMA: Say it properly, Sir Willum.

HAMILTON: You as a Bacchante, by Mr George Romney.

EMMA: Me as a Bacchante, by Sir Joshua Reynolds.

HAMILTON: Less good. Much less good.
He botched the mouth.

EMMA: Me as the Penitent, by Mr George Romney.

HAMILTON: You as Circe, by the same.
The lips were especially good,
Poor man.

EMMA: How he loved me, Sir Willum.
Often he sat there doing nothing
With his brush in the air
Till Mother admonished him.
But that was before your time.
I was still Mr Greville's
He wanted a few of me on the wall
And sent me to Mr Romney in the afternoons.

HAMILTON: That was where I came in.
A dozen were done of you before I came in.

EMMA: Twenty at least
Fifty, a hundred if you count Mr Romney's sketches
His lovesick doodles
Me as a milkmaid, me as Nature
Me as a nymph, often as a nymph...

HAMILTON: A nymph surprised...

EMMA: I was never surprised.
Go on, go on.
What a host there was when I alighted in Naples.

HAMILTON: A frenzy, my love
An upheaval, an earthquake
An exploding Vesuvius of artistic endeavour.

EMMA: Me as Persephone.

HAMILTON: Radiant child.

EMMA: Who by?

HAMILTON: I forget. But I loved you as Flora
By Madame Kaufmann
After an image from under the ash.

EMMA: Ariadne.

HAMILTON: Abandoned.

EMMA: By that devil, your nephew.
Madame Kaufmann again?

HAMILTON: Or Monsieur Tischbein?

EMMA: He did me in Tauris
Longing for Greece
As Iphigenia
And a sibyl, a spirit ascending,
The genius of poesy...

HAMILTON: And by Monsieur Hackert
And Monsieur Rehberg
The other Germans?

EMMA: I forget what as
I begin to forget who by and what as.

HAMILTON: Never mind. You were done.
The image survives:

You as Cassandra, foretelling disaster
You as Euphrosyne.
I suppose it survives. Paint fades,
A canvas burns
Or falls to dolts like the King of Sweden
Who stopped the draughts in his stables with Corregios.
We should have done you oftener in marble,
Agate, carnelian, the hard stones.

EMMA: One for the King
One for Prince Mecklenburg...
Me as Venus in the altogether
Rising from the bath
On a snuffbox for your eyes only.

HAMILTON: Who sees it now?

EMMA: Who sees me now as I was
Fit to be looked at from any angle?

HAMILTON: Fit for Phidias
Fit for Praxiteles
We should have done you more often in marble and bronze.
Evening after evening
My gentlemen looked from the prints in their laps
To you in your shawls on our little stage
And swore that you outdid art. How long
Has the print of you lingered
On their dead retinas?

EMMA: Me as Juno
Me as the mother of Brutus
As Agrippina
As the widow of Mausolus
Faithful.

HAMILTON: Thickening, my love
The ankles, the waist
Heavier and heavier the embonpoint
Even the face
My childish Circe
Slackening, coarsening.
Eight months gone with Lord Nelson's bastard
Nobody knew
But him and me and you.

The gentlemen looked from Sherrards, Gillrays
And the worst, the most savage Rowlandsons
And swore that you outdid art.
A mercy I died when I did
Thin –
It is always a mercy to die thin –
And never saw in the flesh
For the ghost is more than enough
The spread of your last twelve years
The gin and the penury.

EMMA: Me as Aurora, by Madame Lebrun
Me as the Hours
Me as the Muses
Me as the Graces.

HAMILTON: Remember us after the Battle of the Nile
When they did us in wax
The three of us
How large you were
How little the hero was
Half blind, one-armed
And me with the Star and Garter
And longish nose
Looking peaked
When they did us in wax
Tria juncta in uno
And rode us through Naples
Rejoicing
Remember us then?

EMMA: Me as a Vestal
In ivory, that was
Cleopatra
Galatea.

HAMILTON: Ah, Galatea
Whom Pygmalion fashioned
And called her down
Out of the coldness of marble
Into his bed
Where she aged.

EMMA: Who else was there?
Who else was I done as?

Who else was I?
I used to look up at the stars.
Remember, Sir Willum
You taught me the constellations
So many famous females in the stars
Fixed for ever
Will never fatten
Will never go into dust
Such beautiful names
Berenice, her hair
I had lovely hair
A mane of it, auburn
So long, you remember
You made it cover my breasts
Such lovely names
Andromeda
Cassiopea
Me as a naiad
Me as a dryad...

The voices fade.

SCENE FIVE

Joseph and Sir Frederick Treves, Treves pushing Joseph in the wheelchair.

TREVES: Joseph, when you were dead of a broken neck
　　Like a hanged man, that night
　　After the pantomime when perhaps you believed
　　The magic of your own verses had translated you
　　And you let your head fall back like any normal dreaming head
　　Forgetting the weight and it snapped you,
　　We did as you knew we would. I called a sculptress in,
　　One used to East End things, a blonde
　　So pretty you would have sold your soul for her
　　And drew the sheet off you and said she should hurry
　　And do the casts or future humans
　　Would never believe your appearance in the flesh
　　Among us, and she did so. Slimmer than hers
　　And wonderfully delicate was your left arm
　　And the left hand fine and small as a child's
　　When we laid them side by side with the right for comparison.

She had the quick and cultured fingers of a sister of mercy
And worked the plaster firmly over your skull.
Done, it was heavier than she could lift. She worked
Quietly at a table among the skeletons,
Foetuses, tapeworms, hypertrophied organs
And other things in jars, colouring your mouth,
Lending a proper pink to the lopped proboscis,
Transplanting hair and eyebrows for a good likeness.
When this was done and the massive head displayed
Like an ancestor, you fell to me and the knife
As you knew you would, for Science and to aid
Suffering humanity in generations to come.
Heart, poor; lungs, rackety; left hip, tubercular;
Organs of generation in perfect order;
Likewise the brain. This moved me most
Seeing the source of dreams and all that language
Well formed and human in a bony monstrance
Itself turning to stone, to living and vegetating stone,
Growing the way it liked and we did not like.
So I delivered your brain and laid it by
In pickle with what else of you was curious.
When this was done my colleague Openshaw
Boiled you gently in the long vat until
The burdening flesh fell away and you were clean of it.
Then he, famous at this, skilled as Daedalus,
Collected your loose bones and whitened them with peroxide
And piece by piece, over many days and nights,
Articulated you and set you up.

JOSEPH: Thank you.

TREVES: We celebrated when his work was done
And made an occasion with some ceremony
To honour and remember you, as was proper.
Closest staff and colleagues were invited
And Taylor's child who played the fiddle to you,
The sculptress naturally, and of your many visitors
The cream. A sigh went up
Of love and admiration when the curtains opened
And you were shown in a good glass case
Stepping delicately like a very small dinosaur.
So disburdened and as clean as a water baby
How pleased you would have been to see yourself.

Casts of the solid flesh
Were laid around you as though you had risen from them
Like a phoenix, shelled. The sigh we gave
Was of pleasure too, and of relief for you
Such a *tableau vivant*, the poor hip
Throwing you a little forward as though you might run and leap
And the bossy forehead seemed inclining with dreams.
I bowed to Mrs Auberon through the glass.
We had you naked between us as though we met on the tour
In a gallery in Rome and you were the Discus Thrower
Fit to be looked at from any angle
Lasting as long as the world will, in cold marble.
Those were your obsequies, Joseph, and the ceremony.

JOSEPH: Thank you.

TREVES: The lady never visited again.

SCENE SIX

Emma and Joseph, Emma pushing Joseph in his wheelchair.

JOSEPH: You push me nicely, no one better
  Only excepting Mrs Auberon
  In my last days. I had written a pantomime
  With my good left hand
  And I was principal boy but she
  Standing behind me like my inner being
  In top boots and a doublet showing off her figure
  Had to speak my lines
  And circling in the hospital garden
  Towards my last midsummer
  Over my shoulder peeping at the script in my good hand
  Turn by turn she got them word-perfect.

EMMA: I should have had a voice.
  All that dumbshow
  Only the body, see.
  Slim as a sylph
  Fat as Juno
  Then what? A mercy
  Things were loose about the waist in Aphrodite's day.

88

But I should have had a speaking part. To think:
If I'd been later by a hundred years
Like half an hour down here
And you and I had met
Which being so famous the both of us we surely would
You could have had me for your principal boy
And surely would have
Being the best
And made a famous duo.

JOSEPH: It was the story of my life
In verse. To play my mother
I had the prettiest and kindest of the nurses
But Mr Treves said we should have to imagine the elephant.
Seems to me there was a lot they had to imagine:
The change month by month
Under her very eyes
Even within the circle of her arms it couldn't be stopped
And I put on a queer sort of substance
And seemed to be edging into God knows what.
It was a while before they thought of an elephant
All that while wondering
And remembered the circus parade and Mother knocked by one
But I believe they settled for an elephant
And said that was it and that was the reason
And that was the way I was going
Only because that put a name to it
And a sort of limit on what they had to imagine
Since everybody knows what an elephant is
But really no one knew what I was becoming.
I believe they hoped it was only an elephant.
I thank God Mother died
And never saw the enlargement of the mystery.

EMMA: One by a dolt
One by the Hero of the Nile
I was a poor mother to both
But at least the first never saw me.
The second had to watch me die
Inch by inch
Pinched even for gin
It was her little worried face that watched me go.

JOSEPH: She told me stories
    Stroked my thickening arm
    Hushed with her lips against my warping head
    She told me tales
    Again and again and again
    Of Hans the Hedgehog who became a king
    And the youngest brother whose arm was left in feathers
    But he ended well.
    Prince in a frog
    White angel in a rotten tree
    Soul under the soot
    Again and again the secret of life imprisoned
    But always the kiss, the touch,
    The riddle solved, the redeeming word,
    All manner of kindness in the world of nature:
    Healing plants, a deer that led the way,
    A bird alighting on the shoulder with the secret,
    Even the stones
    Edible when most necessary
    So that it seemed to me that if we persevered
    In faith and hope
    There was enough charity strewn around the earth
    For me to hit on metamorphosis
    One fine day.

EMMA: I would have danced you out.
    When I was the nephew's at seventeen
    Or even the uncle's at twenty-one
    I would have danced you into whatever you liked.
    Anything light I was good at then
    Especially Flora
    Especially the girl Persephone
    Surfacing.
    Who would believe it to look at me now?
    Spread as wide as Mammon
    With the ginny face of Polly Nichols
    How queer to think of me in there still
    A chit of a girl
    The dancer
    And all the hundreds I have bodied forth.
    If I could come up again out of this dead flesh
    Whatever you were in yours, Joseph
    I could have danced you out.

JOSEPH: She died. To play the wicked stepmother
    I had Mr Taylor, the chief engineer
    And for the workhouse matron when I fell on the parish
    One of the surgeons volunteered.
    He was a real pantomime dame
    With a rolling pin and bloomers
    He made us laugh
    And there was jollity elsewhere too
    On the road, you know, with the Silver King
    And a quiet scene now and then
    Me in my little caravan reading
    Always reading
    Along the lines Mother taught me
    For it seemed to me that if I worked at the inner being
    I was doing all I could
    And would not be unready when the moment came.
    For that would be a tragedy, sure enough:
    The moment come, the touch, the kiss
    And nothing inside
    Nothing to answer with.
    I saw how many others were waiting just like me
    Waiting in faith and hope
    Under a carapace
    Locked in a filthy den
    Slobbering, mewling or completely dumb
    Raising a hand
    Raising the one good finger of the less bad hand,
    An eyelid. I knew a man, if you can call him that,
    And nothing flickered in him but an eyelid.
    He lifted it
    And he looked out
    And you looked in
    And saw him in there
    Waiting. All this was in my pantomime
    Which grew during the years donated to me
    When the kindness of royalty
    And high society
    And professional men
    And common boys like Mr Taylor's son
    Charlie
    Who played me tunes my mother used to sing
    When all that good
    Collected in my lair in Bedstead Square.

91

EMMA: The body's a wonderful thing when you weigh up.
I stood there weeping over dead Hector
Or mad with love
Unlawfully
For the boy Hippolytus
Or glum at being dumped
By pious Aeneas.
I had more names
Than a poor woman of the streets has customers.
I was the hat and the conjuror as well
Pulling 'em out
No end to it really
Horn of plenty
Bottomless pit
And there was you
Trying your hardest all that time to bring out one of you
One sole self
And do you know something?
Never in all my years did anyone say to me
Do Emma for a change
Your sole self
Do her
And if they had've could I have?
But you had a good idea of it at least
The inner thing, I mean
The soul
And only wanted body.

JOSEPH: For the one performance of my pantomime
I wore my Sunday best
A decent three-piece cut to accommodate my shape
With fob and chain
And a clean white handkerchief in my breast pocket.
I was silent in my special chair
With Mrs Auberon behind me as my alter ego
Speaking the lines
And wheeling me through the action.
Often she laid a hand on my worse shoulder.

EMMA: Like this?

JOSEPH: Just so. It was midsummer.
Often in the delivery of my lines
She leaned

And the ungiving bosses of my skull
Were cushioned against the woman in her boyish costume.

EMMA: Like this?

JOSEPH: Exactly so.
I will not pretend that the hospital was silent.
The cries arrived from the receiving ward
And the streets pressed in as murderously as ever
For the long warm evenings
Excite desires in the poor people
And they have nothing to quieten them
Nothing to hand in their soiled territory
Only harm, the doing and suffering,
They see that what they want they will not have
And curse God for the glimpses.
But we acted the story of my life from the beginning
Before an audience who could bear to look at me
On the mild midsummer night
In the company of the fountain and the scent of stocks.
Wheel me as she did, will you?

EMMA: In among the scenes.

JOSEPH: It was like a picture book.

EMMA: The circus parade.
Imagine the elephant.

JOSEPH: Turning the pages
And Charlie Taylor played us a tune for each
So many tunes in such a little fellow
He seemed to have them as the fountain has
Eternal water
And gave them out
God bless him.

EMMA: You in the fairy stories.

JOSEPH: As Mother told them.

EMMA: You as a little matchboy.
You in the workhouse.

JOSEPH: Me on the road with the other novelties.

EMMA: You in your cloak and cap and veil
All of a heap
In the waiting room on Liverpool Street Station.

JOSEPH: Me underground
  Safe and sound
  Clean and spruce
  Sitting up for my hours of conversation
  In Bedstead Square.

EMMA: And I was your favourite visitor
  The young and pretty widow Mrs Auberon
  And what you said
  I felt the deeper meaning
  Behind what Mr Treves allowed.

JOSEPH: There was nothing you did not understand.
  You took my hand.

EMMA: Like this.

JOSEPH: Your face when you lifted your veil
  Came over mine like the pitying moon
  Come out from a cloud
  Inclining. How many hours all told
  Of bathing in the moonlight of your face
  Before you washed me clean?

*Dreamy interlude in which the idyllic and sentimental tones of Joseph's
life are heard as nightingales, the fountain, Charlie's violin etc. Then,
quite abruptly,*

EMMA: How did it end?

JOSEPH: The ending was beautiful.
  My verse lifted.
  I had steeped myself in the stories
  And had devised an ending
  In which I vanished or
  In the eyes of those who had borne the sight of me
  Was metamorphosed. It was easy to arrange.
  I beguiled the audience with a dreamy interlude
  In which the feelings of a liberated soul
  Occurred to them in images and singing
  And all the while my speaker
  The living image of my cleanly self
  Stepping backwards
  Withdrew me out of the light
  Until we were in shadow against the railings

Against the iron gate for which I had my key
And there I exited unseen
Wheeling myself away
And Mrs Auberon stepped into the light again
And stood for me.
Imagine her appearance
Tall, slim and beautiful
The principal boy
The prince
Arms lifting a little
Smiling
Silent, but saying
See me
Fit to be looked at.
What a finale!

EMMA: Like this? See me
See I stand in for her
Slim as a wraith
Girlish, the dancer
The risen springtime
Unspoilt
Beginning again.

JOSEPH: Wheeling myself away the best I could
Under the walls of those unforgivable streets
I heard the applause behind me
Heartfelt, louder and louder
Overwhelming while it lasted
The rattle of the streets and wards and my
Hard won breath.

Fades into the dry whispering with which the play began.

David Constantine was born in 1944 in Salford, Lancashire. He read Modern Languages at Wadham College, Oxford, and from 1969 to 1981 was a lecturer in German at Durham University. He is now Fellow in German at the Queen's College, Oxford. He is married with two children, and lives in Oxford.

His first book of poems, *A Brightness to Cast Shadows* (Bloodaxe Books, 1980), was widely acclaimed. His second collection, *Watching for Dolphins* (Bloodaxe Books, 1983), won the 1984 Alice Hunt Bartlett Prize, and his academic study, *Early Greek Travellers and the Hellenic Ideal* (Cambridge University Press, 1984), won the first Runciman Prize in 1985. His first novel, *Davies*, was published by Bloodaxe in 1985, and his first book of stories, *Back at the Spike* by Ryburn Publishing in 1994.

His third collection, *Madder* (Bloodaxe Books, 1987), a Poetry Book Society Recommendation, won the Southern Arts Literature Prize. The French edition of *Madder*, translated by Yves Bichet as *Sorlingues* (Éditions La Dogana, 1992), won the Prix Rhône-Alpes du Livre. His *Selected Poems* (Bloodaxe Books, 1991) is a Poetry Book Society Recommendation. His latest collections are *Caspar Hauser: a poem in nine cantos* (Bloodaxe Books, 1994) and *The Pelt of Wasps* (Bloodaxe Books, 1998), which includes his verse-play *Lady Hamilton and the Elephant Man*, first broadcast on BBC Radio 3 in 1997.

He has published a critical introduction to the poetry of Friedrich Hölderlin (Oxford University Press, 1988), and a translation of Hölderlin's *Selected Poems* (Bloodaxe Books, 1990; new edition, 1996). He has also translated Goethe's novel *Elective Affinities* (Oxford University Press, World's Classics, 1994) and Kleist's *Selected Writings* (Dent, 1997). The Bloodaxe Contemporary French Poets series includes his translations of (with Helen Constantine) *Spaced, Displaced* by Henri Michaux (1992) and (with Mark Treharne) *Under Clouded Skies / Beauregard* by Philippe Jaccottet (1994).